974.2 BRO
35248000850374
2
Br               1957-
N

DISCARDED                '04

P9-ELR-748

OAK CREEK (WISCONSIN) PUBLIC LIBRARY

# NEW HAMPSHIRE

# NEW HAMPSHIRE

HELLO
U.S.A.

by Dottie Brown

OAK CREEK (WISCONSIN) PUBLIC LIBRARY

Lerner Publications Company

*You'll find this picture of granite at the beginning of each chapter in this book. New Hampshire's hills and mountains contain large amounts of granite. The mining of this stone has long been an important industry in the state. New Hampshirites have honored granite as their official state rock.*

Cover (left): White Mountains National Forest. Cover (right): Ice climbing in the White Mountains. Pages 2–3: Winter in a village near Manchester. Page 3: Harvested pumpkins for sale.

Copyright © 2002 by Lerner Publications Company

All rights reserved. International copyright secured. No part of this book may be reproduced, stored in a retrieval system, or transmitted in any form or by any means—electronic, mechanical, photocopying, recording, or otherwise—without the prior written permission of Lerner Publications Company, except for the inclusion of brief quotations in an acknowledged review.

*This book is available in two editions:*
Library binding by Lerner Publications Company, a division of Lerner Publishing Group
Soft cover by First Avenue Editions, an imprint of Lerner Publishing Group
241 First Avenue North
Minneapolis, MN 55401 U.S.A.

Website address: www.lernerbooks.com

Library of Congress Cataloging-in-Publication Data

Brown, Dottie, 1957–
    New Hampshire / by Dottie Brown. (Rev. and expanded 2nd ed.)
        p.   cm. — (Hello U.S.A.)
    Includes index.
    Summary: An introduction to the land, history, people, economy, and environment of New Hampshire.
        ISBN: 0–8225–4086–X (lib. bdg. : alk. paper)
        ISBN: 0–8225–0788–9 (pbk. : alk. paper)
        1. New Hampshire—Juvenile literature. [1. New Hampshire.] I. Title.
    II. Series.
    F34.3 .B76 2002
    974.2—dc21                                                            2001006408

Manufactured in the United States of America
1 2 3 4 5 6 – JR – 07  06  05  04  03  02

# CONTENTS

New Hampshire's rocky hills are covered by forests.

# THE LAND

## The Granite State

Perched atop one of New Hampshire's many rocky peaks, the Old Man of the Mountains overlooks the countryside. Huge granite rocks collided thousands of years ago and shaped the figure, also known as Great Stone Face. Over time, people living in the area have passed along stories about the face. Great Stone Face has become part of the reason for New Hampshire's nickname—the Granite State.

Granite—a hard rock known for its strength and beauty—is a symbol of New Hampshire. The state's many mountains and hills are filled with granite. Thick, green forests cover most of the Granite State's rocky landscape.

Old Man of the Mountains

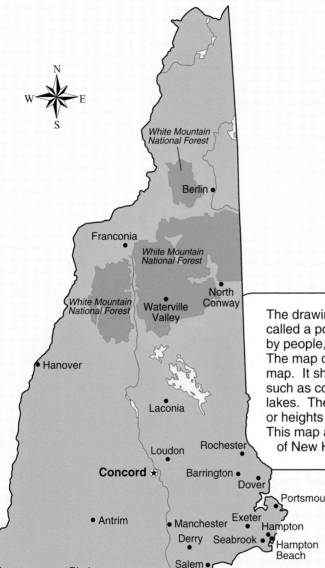

## NEW HAMPSHIRE
## Political Map

⭐ State capital

```
0        10       20 Miles
0  10  20  30  40 Kilometers
```

White Mountain
National Forest

Berlin

Franconia

White Mountain
National Forest

White Mountain
National Forest

Waterville
Valley

North
Conway

Hanover

Laconia

Loudon

Rochester

Concord ⭐

Barrington

Dover

Portsmouth

Antrim

Exeter

Manchester

Hampton

Derry

Seabrook

Hampton
Beach

Salem

Rindge

Nashua

The drawing of New Hampshire on this page is called a political map. It shows features created by people, including cities, railways, and parks. The map on the facing page is called a physical map. It shows physical features of New Hampshire, such as coasts, islands, mountains, rivers, and lakes. The colors represent a range of elevations, or heights above sea level (see legend box). This map also shows the geographical regions of New Hampshire.

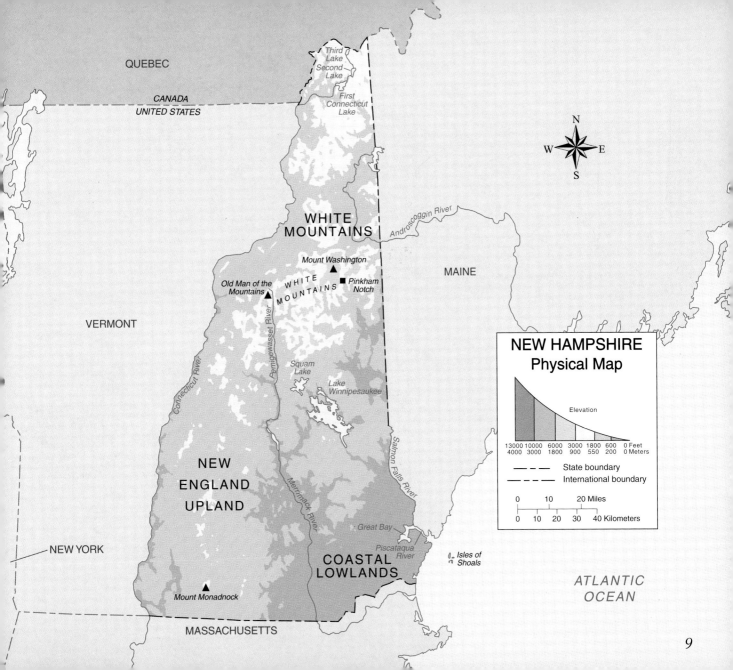

QUEBEC

CANADA
UNITED STATES

*Third Lake*
*Second Lake*
*First Connecticut Lake*

N
W E
S

WHITE
MOUNTAINS

*Androscoggin River*

*Mount Washington* ▲

MAINE

*Old Man of the Mountains* ▲

WHITE
MOUNTAINS

■ *Pinkham Notch*

VERMONT

*Pemigewasset River*

*Connecticut River*

*Squam Lake*

*Lake Winnipesaukee*

## NEW HAMPSHIRE
### Physical Map

Elevation

| 13000 | 10000 | 6000 | 3000 | 1800 | 600 | 0 Feet |
| 4000 | 3000 | 1800 | 900 | 550 | 200 | 0 Meters |

‒ ‒ ‒   State boundary

— — —   International boundary

| 0 | 10 | 20 Miles |

| 0 | 10 | 20 | 30 | 40 Kilometers |

NEW
ENGLAND
UPLAND

*Merrimack River*

*Salmon Falls River*

*Great Bay*

*Piscataqua River*

NEW YORK

COASTAL
LOWLANDS

ι. *Isles of Shoals*

ATLANTIC
OCEAN

▲
*Mount Monadnock*

MASSACHUSETTS

9

Nestled in the northeastern corner of the United States, New Hampshire is part of New England. The state is shaped like a slender triangle. Maine and the Atlantic Ocean border New Hampshire on the east. Vermont is New Hampshire's neighbor to the west. Massachusetts forms the base of the triangle and Canada borders the northern tip.

Fire and ice sculpted the land long before people ever lived in New Hampshire. More than 100 million years ago, pressures inside the earth forced up **lava,** or blazing, melted rock, to the earth's surface. As time passed, the rock hardened into slabs. **Glaciers**—huge, slowly moving sheets of ice—marched across the rocky land millions of years later.

As they pushed south, the glaciers shaped much of the land in the Granite State. The massive ice sheets carved out valleys, wore down mountains, and scratched out lake beds. By the time the glaciers melted, they had molded the three land regions in New Hampshire—the Coastal Lowlands, the New England Upland, and the White Mountains.

The Coastal Lowlands are comprised partly of offshore islands *(left)*. A small town is cradled in the hills of the New England Upland *(below)*.

The Coastal Lowlands cover the southeastern corner of New Hampshire. This region stretches about 20 miles inland from the Atlantic Ocean. Sandy beaches blanket parts of the region's winding shoreline. Portsmouth, which lies near the coast, is the state's only shipping port.

The New England Upland extends over the rest of the southern half of the state. It is known for its many lakes, trees, and rolling hills. Some of New Hampshire's most fertile farmland lies in the region. And much of the state's granite is mined in the New England Upland, near the city of Concord.

The White Mountains
sometimes harbor
sudden storms.

The White Mountains region extends north of the
New England Upland.  Tall mountains cover most of
the region, but the slopes flatten out near the
Canadian border.  Six peaks in the White
Mountains, all named after U.S. presidents, rise
more than one mile into the sky.

High in the White Mountains, many streams begin their tumbling course down the slopes. The Pemigewasset River forms here, near the Old Man of the Mountains. It flows south into the Merrimack River.

The Connecticut River, which begins near the northern tip of the state, separates New Hampshire from Vermont. The Androscoggin River rushes through thick forests in northeastern New Hampshire before entering Maine. Many small rivers and streams flow into Great Bay, a large body of salt water connected to the Atlantic Ocean by the Piscataqua River.

New Hampshire has many lakes— about 1,300 in all. The largest lakes, including Winnipesaukee and Squam, lie in the New England Upland. Near the state's northern boundary, the Connecticut Lakes lead up into Canada.

Pemigewasset River

The Atlantic Ocean creates a big difference between the climate near New Hampshire's coast and that of the rest of the state. In the winter, the ocean holds in heat and keeps the air fairly warm near the coast. Temperatures there hover around 25° F. Higher up, in the White Mountains, the air can be chilling. Here, the temperature can plunge far below zero. New Hampshire's summers tend to be dry and cool, with temperatures averaging about 70° F.

Most of New Hampshire's **precipitation** (rain, snow, sleet, and hail) comes in the form of snow. More than 100 inches of

New Hampshire's snowy mountainsides are great for skiing.

A forest in fall color
on Mount Morgan in
central New Hampshire

snow fall in the mountains each year, but the coast gets much less. In the summer, most parts of New Hampshire receive 10 to 15 inches of rain.

All that precipitation provides plenty of water for New Hampshire's trees. More than 84 percent of the state is wooded. Oak, sugar maple, beech, and birch trees grow alongside pines, spruces, and cedars. Flowering shrubs, violets, and fireweeds add color to the state's landscape. New Hampshire's state flower, the purple lilac, blossoms in the lowlands.

The state's woodlands are home to many kinds of animals. Black bears roam far in the north, and moose there feed on shrubs and water plants. Deer, chipmunks, mink, and foxes scamper throughout the state's countryside. Loons, ducks, and geese nest near lakeshores. Coastal waters shelter lobsters, oysters, and shrimp.

Two curious New Hampshire animals: a moose *(right)* and a little fox pup *(below)*

# THE HISTORY

## Natives and Newcomers

The first people to live near the Atlantic coast were American Indians, or Native Americans, who settled in the area thousands of years ago. By the year A.D. 1500, the Pennacook—descendants of the earliest Indians—were the main tribe living in the woodlands of what later became New Hampshire. The Pennacook and neighboring Indians shared similar customs and understood each other's languages.

Pennacook villages housed 50 to 200 people. Families lived in dome-shaped wigwams, which the women built. They made frames from the branches of young, flexible trees and covered the frames with bark. To keep warm in the winter, the Indians lined the walls of the wigwams with fur.

Pennacook Indians crafted canoes to help them travel the waterways in what would become New Hampshire.

Corn husks and corn silk were used to make dolls for Pennacook children.

Pennacook women also farmed small plots of land, growing pumpkins, squashes, beans, and corn. With their children, the women gathered strawberries, raspberries, blueberries, currants, and nuts from the woods. They sewed clothes out of soft deer hides and decorated them with seashells, paint, feathers, and dyed porcupine quills. Using bows and arrows, the men hunted deer, moose, beavers, and birds. They also built canoes for travel and speared fish from the rivers and lakes.

During New Hampshire's chilly winters, the Indians wrapped themselves in warm furs. To travel easily across deep snow, they wore snowshoes. The men hunted wild game and went ice fishing for trout. The Indians also ate pemmican—a mixture of dried berries and smoked meats preserved for the cold season.

When spring arrived, the Pennacook tapped the sap from sugar maple trees, boiling it to make maple sugar and syrup. The Indians also watched the budding oak trees carefully. When the oak leaves were as big as a mouse's ear, the Pennacook knew it was time to plant corn.

The Pennacook used branches and leather to make snowshoes.

Captain John Smith

European explorers first visited Pennacook territory in the early 1600s. King James I of Great Britain had heard of the area's lush forests and its good fishing from John Smith. Smith was a British captain who had explored much of the Atlantic coast. The king claimed this land for Britain, and his son Prince Charles named it New England.

In 1622 King James granted a large chunk of New England to two wealthy noblemen, Captain John Mason and Sir Ferdinando Gorges. Several groups of British people went to live on the newly claimed land. The settlers built several villages, forming a **colony,** or settlement, which was ruled by Great Britain.

Mason and Gorges named their properties in 1629. Mason named his colony New Hampshire. Gorges's portion became Maine.

Mason and Gorges split up their land in 1629. Mason named his portion New Hampshire, after Hampshire County, his homeland in Britain. By 1640 the colony of New Hampshire had four towns—Portsmouth, Exeter, Dover, and Hampton.

New Hampshire's settlers traded British shirts, blankets, kettles, axes, and knives to the Indians for furs and fish. Ships carried the furs and dried fish back to Great Britain, where people were eager to buy them. The settlers also cut down rows and rows of trees. Shipbuilders used the colony's vast wood supply to make ships for Britain's navy.

With the help of Native Americans, New Hampshire's settlers began to feel at home. The Indians taught the settlers how to farm, how to catch wild game, and how to find plants that were good for food and medicines.

But contact with the Europeans changed the Indians' way of life. The Pennacook grew dependent on trading with the settlers. By the late 1600s, the Indians had stopped making some of their own goods.

Europeans used beaver fur to make hats.

As the settlers' villages grew, New Hampshire's wilderness also changed. Settlers cut down more forests for lumber and to make room for farmland. Without trees and brush to live in, many wild animals fled to find new shelter. As a result, the Indians in New Hampshire had to travel farther to hunt game animals.

Sawdust from the colonists' lumber mills polluted the water in nearby rivers. The colonists had also built dams across rivers to form **reservoirs**—large pools of water—for everyday use. The dams slowed the water's flow, and many fish died in the dirty, slow-moving water. Soon there were fewer fish for the Pennacook to catch. The Indians grew angry about all of these changes.

Tree stumps were very difficult to remove. Early colonists often planted their crops around them.

# Passaconaway

Chief Passaconaway was an Indian sachem, or leader, in the 1600s. His name meant "Child of the Bear." Passaconaway led the Pennacook Confederacy, a group of Pennacook tribes in parts of what later became New Hampshire, Maine, and Massachusetts. Like many other Indians, he caught a disease brought to America by the Europeans. These new diseases killed thousands of Indians. Only 1 out of every 20 Indians, mostly Pennacook, in New Hampshire and Vermont were spared from disease in the 1600s.

Even on his deathbed, Passaconaway was thinking about the future of his people. When the Indians began feuding with British colonists, the wise chief worried that a war would destroy the Pennacook. Passaconaway urged the Pennacook to keep peace with the settlers, but the battles that had begun did not end for many years. According to legend, after Passaconaway died, a pack of mighty wolves pulled his body on a sled to the top of Mount Washington. There, Passaconaway disappeared in a cloud of fire.

By 1689 Great Britain had colonies along much of the Atlantic coast. The British also claimed land west of these settlements, thinking they would find even more fish, furs, and lumber there.

Meanwhile, the French had established many trading posts to the north and to the west of New Hampshire. Like the British, the French made lots of money selling the furs they got from the Native Americans. The French wanted to control the fur trade throughout North America, and they were willing to fight the British for it.

By the late 1600s, French traders knew of the problems Native Americans were having with the British. Wanting the Indians on their side, the French encouraged them to attack British colonists. In response to the attacks, New Hampshire and other colonies offered a reward for the scalp of any Indian—man, woman, or child.

The series of battles involving the French, British, and Indians—called the French and Indian War— finally ended in 1763 with a British victory. Many Pennacook had been killed in battle. Others had died from diseases they had caught from the colonists. The survivors fled to Canada, where French settlers were friendly to most Indians.

To help pay for the French and Indian War, Great Britain raised taxes in its 13 North American colonies, including New Hampshire. The high taxes made the colonists very angry. The Americans did not like Britain telling them what to do, so they decided to fight for independence.

In colonial times, the British used this fort in battles against the French and the Indians. The fort has been restored to look like it did during that time period.

Built in Portsmouth, the *Ranger* was the first U.S. ship to hoist the Stars and Stripes.

The war for independence, called the American Revolution, broke out in 1775. New Hampshire sent hundreds of men to Boston to fight the British soldiers. In January 1776, New Hampshire adopted its own **constitution,** or written set of basic laws. With this document, New Hampshire became the first colony to form a government separate from Great Britain.

After the colonies won the war in 1783, they wrote a constitution for the United States of America. On June 21, 1788, New Hampshire became the ninth state to sign the U.S. Constitution and join the new nation.

By this time, more than 140,000 settlers lived in New Hampshire. Many families had small farms, which were clustered around villages. Farmers cleared the land to plant fields of wheat, corn, peas, pumpkins, and oats. Women spun yarn, wove cloth, and sewed the family's clothes. Families made soap from scratch, dipped their own candles, wove baskets and rugs, and sewed quilts.

In the villages, blacksmiths hammered away on nails, hooks, and horseshoes. Millers ground corn and wheat. Tanners prepared animal hides for leather shoes and saddles. Money was scarce, so townsfolk often bartered, or traded, for goods and services. For example, farmers might trade part of their corn crop to the miller in exchange for having the rest of the crop ground into cornmeal.

Blacksmiths pound melted iron into horseshoes.

In the early 1800s, industries began to grow in New Hampshire. Granite mining began to supply material for many U.S. buildings. Settlers also had learned to create **hydropower,** or energy from flowing water, by building dams across rivers. The dams held back the water, which was then released

The stone quarries, or mines, near Concord supplied tons of granite to builders in the 1800s.

through large wheels. The force of the water was used to power machines in mills. Soon, cloth mills sprang up alongside the state's swift rivers and streams.

As industry grew, transportation improved. In 1838 New Hampshire opened its first railroad. Trains began to transport goods to markets in other states. Railroads made it easy for lumber companies to reach the vast forests of New Hampshire's White Mountains. Crews of 30 men or more would camp among the trees, cutting down huge areas of forest before moving on. Loggers floated timber down rivers or sent it by train to lumber and paper mills.

Many products went by train to Portsmouth, which had become a leading port and shipbuilding town. From Portsmouth, ships packed with U.S. products sailed to Europe. And ships from other countries docked at the busy port to unload their cargo.

Lumber was transported down the Connecticut River from New Hampshire's northern woods.

Daniel Webster

The state's traders and manufacturers had Daniel Webster, a New Hampshire politician, to fight for laws in their favor. While working for the U.S. government, Webster influenced lawmakers, presidents, and judges. People throughout the United States listened to what he had to say.

Webster's most important struggle affected the entire nation. In the 1830s, some people wanted the states to have laws more powerful than the nation's laws. But Webster fought for strong national laws, fearing that a weak U.S. government would not be able to hold the young country together.

By 1850 many more Americans were worried about national unity. In the Southern states, many people used slaves from Africa to work in the fields and to do other hard work. In New Hampshire, as in all Northern states, slavery was illegal. When politicians tried to outlaw slavery throughout the nation, the Southern states threatened to leave the Union, or United States.

Daniel Webster was against slavery, but his main goal was to keep the nation together. Webster helped pass the Compromise of 1850, a series of laws about slavery that he hoped both Northerners and Southerners could agree on.

Town meetings, where issues such as national unity might be discussed, were usually held in town halls. Many such buildings were built in New Hampshire in the 1800s.

The Compromise of 1850 helped calm the nation for a while, but people continued to argue about slavery. By 1854 the United States had claimed almost all of the territory between Mexico and Canada. As people moved west to buy land, questions arose about whether to allow slavery in new territories. Northerners wanted to outlaw slavery in the territories, but Southerners wanted it legalized.

The territories of Kansas and Nebraska were in the center of the slavery debate in the mid-1800s.

The Kansas-Nebraska Act of 1854 said that settlers in the two new territories could decide for themselves whether or not to permit slavery. This act was signed into law by U.S. president Franklin Pierce, another New Hampshirite.

Northerners became very angry about the law, and arguments between the North and the South grew into the Civil War (1861–1865). During this war, the Southern states formed a separate country and fought against the Northern states. The North won the war in 1865, and the nation was once again united.

These young women worked in a New Hampshire textile (cloth) mill in the late 1800s.

After the Civil War, New Hampshire's growing factories needed more and more workers. Thousands of **immigrants** from Europe and Canada came to New Hampshire for jobs. By 1874 more than half of New Hampshire's workers were employed in manufacturing. The state's products included everything from shoes and books to glass and pianos.

Industry boomed even more in 1917, when the United States entered World War I (1914–1918). To supply the nation's soldiers, workers produced weapons, leather boots, and cloth for uniforms.

In this 1906 picture, textile workers, including children, leave the Amoskeag Manufacturing Company at the end of the day.

## Manchester's Mammoth Mills

By the early 1900s, the Amoskeag Manufacturing Company in Manchester had become the largest textile factory in the world. At its peak, the company operated 30 mills and employed about 17,000 workers. The company owed its size in part to the unusual way it began. First, planners built rows and rows of mills below the Amoskeag Falls of the Merrimack River. The city of Manchester was then designed around the company's buildings.

Thousands of people moved to Manchester to find work in the growing company, bringing along their unique cloth-making skills. The Scots, for example, were experts at making checkered cloth known as gingham. Sometimes entire families worked in the mills. Young boys and girls often cleaned or ran the thread-making machines. Women were usually weavers or cloth inspectors, and men operated the heavy machinery. On busy days, the company's workers turned out more than 50 miles of cloth per hour.

In the late 1920s, the Amoskeag Manufacturing Company began losing money. By 1936 the mills had closed down, leaving thousands of people jobless. Although it later recovered from the loss of the mills, the city of Manchester faced years of poverty. The cloth-making machines at the Amoskeag Company have been silent for many years. But the gigantic factory buildings still stand, reminding residents of Manchester's past.

Businesses throughout the United States suffered during the Great Depression of the 1930s. Many Americans lost their jobs and had very little money to spend. Because people could not afford to buy New Hampshire's products, factories in the state struggled to stay open.

The outbreak of World War II in 1939 gave a new boost to many U.S. businesses. Factories in New Hampshire again supplied the military with items such as parachutes, uniforms, weapons, and submarines. The state also sent many soldiers overseas to fight in the war.

The northern New Hampshire town of Berlin grew rapidly in the early 1900s. Its growth was assisted by new railroads and paved roads for automobiles.

After the war ended in 1945, New Hampshire advertised throughout the country, encouraging people to spend their vacations in the Granite State. More and more visitors traveled to New Hampshire to hike in the mountain forests and to sunbathe on the beaches. In the 1970s, new industries came to the state. Many New Hampshirites began to make computers and electrical parts.

Throughout the 1990s and into the 2000s, New Hampshire's technology industry has continued to grow. It ranks high among the nation's manufacturers of computers and other electronics. The state is also a leader in financial services, such as banking and insurance.

New Hampshirites once depended mainly on furs, fish, and lumber for survival. By embracing technology and the future it holds, people in the state have since found new ways to make a living. New Hampshirites have shown that their determination to succeed is set in stone as hard as granite.

Workers at this factory in New Hampshire are storing fiber optic cable, a thin thread of glass that carries telephone, television, and Internet signals.

# PEOPLE & ECONOMY

## A Rich Heritage

N ew Hampshire is one of the country's smallest states, and its small population matches its size. About 1.2 million people call New Hampshire home, ranking it 41st of the 50 states in population.

Many New Hampshirites have ancestors who came from Great Britain during New Hampshire's days as a British colony. Some people trace their roots back to other European countries. About one-fourth of New Hampshire's residents are descendants of French Canadians who moved to the United States in the 1800s. Latinos, African Americans, and Asian Americans make up nearly 4 percent of the state's population.

About 40,000 people live in the capital city of Concord.

Slightly more than half of New Hampshire's residents live in cities, most of which are small. Manchester, New Hampshire's largest city, is home to over 100,000 people. Nashua, Concord (the state capital), Derry, and Rochester are the next largest cities.

New Hampshire's cities and countryside offer many exciting things to see and do. Racing fans watch cars and motorcycles zip around the track at the New Hampshire International Speedway in Loudon. Champion dogs race in Seabrook Greyhound Park, and racehorses compete at Rockingham Park in Salem. During the winter, a handful of world skiing championships takes place in the White Mountains. New Hampshirites close each summer with an annual seafood festival at Hampton Beach.

Fairs throughout New Hampshire feature lumberjack competitions.

New Hampshire's historical sites attract many modern explorers. In the center of Portsmouth, Strawbery Banke has been restored to look the way it did during its days as a colonial seaport. The Cog Railway, in the northern part of the state, takes brave riders up and down the hair-raising slopes of Mount Washington. There, visitors can see Old Peppersass—the first train used on the railway—and peek at the weather dials in the Sherman Adams Summit Building.

With hundreds of parks and forests, New Hampshire is a perfect place for lovers of the great outdoors. Adventures range from scaling Mount Monadnock to camping at Moose Brook State Park.

New Hampshire's White Mountains are a popular spot for hikers.

A cross-country skier *(left)* follows a trail through the New Hampshire Audubon Society's Thompson Sanctuary. A sailboarder *(above)* glides across Little Dublin Pond.

Photographers and hikers hope to spot some of the state's wildlife. Swift rivers, large lakes, and coastal waters test the skills of boaters, fishers, and swimmers. And during the cold season, snowmobilers, snowboarders, and skiers race through New Hampshire's deep snow.

A school bus passes through one of New Hampshire's many covered bridges.

All these outdoor attractions make tourism a big business in New Hampshire. The industry brings nearly $10 billion into the state each year. Thousands of New Hampshirites have service jobs, working to assist visitors in parks and resorts. Workers also serve as guides, innkeepers, and waitpeople.

Altogether, almost two-thirds of the state's workers—66 percent—have some type of service job. Besides helping tourists, service workers in New Hampshire sell everyday products such as food, clothing, and gasoline. Doctors, bankers, and mechanics provide other important services to people in New Hampshire. About 14 percent of New Hampshirites work for the government. Government workers at the state's weather research center atop Mount Washington provide weather information to the National Weather Service, to the U.S. Army, and to engineers around the nation.

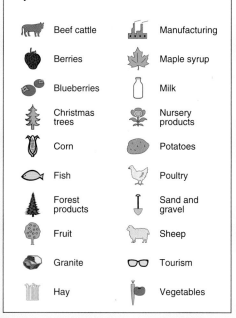

# NEW HAMPSHIRE
## Economic Map

The symbols on this map show where different economic activities take place in New Hampshire. The legend below explains what each symbol stands for.

| Symbol | Name | Symbol | Name |
|---|---|---|---|
| | Beef cattle | | Manufacturing |
| | Berries | | Maple syrup |
| | Blueberries | | Milk |
| | Christmas trees | | Nursery products |
| | Corn | | Potatoes |
| | Fish | | Poultry |
| | Forest products | | Sand and gravel |
| | Fruit | | Sheep |
| | Granite | | Tourism |
| | Hay | | Vegetables |

One of every five jobholders in New Hampshire works in manufacturing. Unlike the factories of the past, many of the state's modern industries specialize in high technology. Many residents of New Hampshire put together computers, electrical equipment, and scientific instruments. Leather and plastic products also are manufactured in New Hampshire.

Manufacturers in New Hampshire make everything from barrels *(left)* to computers. Sweet syrups and candies are made from maple tree sap *(above)*.

Using a potter's wheel, a New Hampshire potter shapes a clay vase.

The state's many craft-workers take pride in producing handmade items much like those made in colonial days. Lamps, jewelry, rugs, wicker baskets, pottery, quilts, and pewter candlesticks fill shops throughout the state. New Hampshirites also make and sell fresh maple syrup, jellies, and relishes.

New Hampshire's forests provide the raw materials for wooden products and paper goods. Loggers cut down trees and haul the wood to lumber and paper mills. Much of the wood is sawed into lumber for building houses and making furniture. At paper mills, machines roll out writing paper and process paper bags and paper towels. Other workers print magazines and newspapers.

Some mining still goes on in New Hampshire. Miners scoop up sand, crush stones into gravel, and carve granite from the state's mountains and hills. Sand and gravel are used for making roads and concrete. The granite is shipped throughout the United States to be used in construction.

New Hampshire's lumber and rock are used to build buildings and homes.

In the late 1800s, half the people who lived in New Hampshire farmed the land. But as other New Hampshire industries have grown, only 2 percent of the state's workers earn a living from farming. Most farmers raise dairy cows, but some have beef cattle, hogs, and poultry. Farmers grow more hay than any other crop, using it to feed New Hampshire's cattle. Some farmers specialize in apples, the state's leading fruit crop.

Northern New Hampshire is home to Christmas tree farms.

New Hampshire continues to grow and change, but the joy its residents take in their state stays the same. These costumed New Hampshirites celebrate autumn at a fall harvest festival.

In some ways, New Hampshire has changed a great deal over the past three centuries. By focusing on financial services and the high-tech industry, the state is leading the way into the future. But New Hampshire has also kept its ties to the past. The traditional industries of farming and logging still play an important role in New Hampshire's success.

# THE ENVIRONMENT

## Protecting the Wilderness

 or hundreds of years, New Hampshire's population grew very slowly. In 1950, after more than 160 years of statehood, only 500,000 people lived in New Hampshire. But in the year 2000, the state's population was more than double that number. And though New Hampshire has fewer residents per square mile than many other states, its population is on the rise.

Many people come to New Hampshire to enjoy its scenic beauty.

In recent decades, more and more people have moved to New Hampshire. They want to enjoy the state's fresh air, scenic countryside, sparkling rivers, and abundant forests. The newcomers provide New Hampshire with more workers, who help the state earn more money. But a higher population can also threaten the state's environment.

The increasing numbers of visitors and residents of New Hampshire *(right)* create an increasing amount of garbage *(below).*

New condominiums
and ski areas bring
more and more
vacationers to the
mountains each winter.

   The 1980s were a time of huge
growth for New Hampshire. During
the middle years of that decade, new
homes, factories, roads, and office
buildings swallowed up 20,000 acres
of New Hampshire's forests and farmland a year. These built-up areas, or
**developments,** spread out over more
and more land, increasing air pollution
and garbage in the state. Worried
about losing the state's wilderness and countryside
areas, New Hampshirites began looking for ways to
keep some of the land clean and unspoiled.

Within two years, this pasture was transformed into a housing development.

Starting in the mid-1980s, New Hampshire managed a program to help preserve some of the land. Millions of dollars from government, businesses, and individuals helped support the program. The money was used to pay landowners to sign a contract, or agreement, promising not to build or make major changes on certain areas of land. In the mid-1990s, contracts preserved more than 127,000 acres of the state's forests, parks, lakeshores, and farmland.

Because more than 84 percent of the state is forested, many of the contracts are on forests. The rules in these contracts protect woodlands in many ways. Some rules ban motor vehicles, which damage the soft floor of the forest. Others forbid mining on the land.

But contracts on forests do allow logging. New Hampshire's lumber and wood industry adds nearly $250 million to the state's earnings each year. Many landowners would have refused to sign a contract if it had kept them from using this valuable natural resource.

Farming *(left)* and logging *(above)* can still take place on most of the lands preserved by contracts.

Loggers supply lumber for many industries, including the paper mills in Berlin, New Hampshire.

Some New Hampshirites feel that the contract program is not enough to save the state's woodlands. Many of these citizens work on projects to help control the type, amount, and location of trees cut down in New Hampshire's forests. And they try to make sure that enough new trees are planted to replace those cut down by loggers. Some residents, concerned about losing the wooded habitats of New Hampshire's birds and animals, would like to end logging in much of the state.

Other environmental issues have created arguments in New Hampshire. One issue was the building of a nuclear power plant at Seabrook Beach near the Atlantic coast. Those in favor of the plant were looking forward to the inexpensive energy the plant would provide. But the Seabrook

project drew angry opposition from environment-alists. They were concerned an accident at the nuclear reactor could cause great damage to both the wilderness and the populated areas. A demon-stration against the construction of the plant led to the arrest of 1,400 protesters in 1977. However, despite the protests, the Seabrook plant became operational in 1990. It is the last nuclear power plant built in the United States.

The Seabrook nuclear power plant under construction. Some New Hampshirites were concerned about building a nuclear facility in their state.

Residents of New Hampshire hope that some of the state's wilderness areas will remain undisturbed by its growing population.

New Hampshirites are also teaching their children to take care of the Granite State's land, hoping to preserve it far into the future. By working together, the state's residents can tackle the challenge of caring for the land as more and more people move into the state. The Old Man of the Mountains—watching over the state with his granite stare—reminds New Hampshirites of the beauty of the state they are proud to call home.

New Hampshirite students learn about trees and their importance to wildlife.

# ALL ABOUT NEW HAMPSHIRE

## Fun Facts

**In 1934 workers at Mount Washington's** weather observatory in New Hampshire witnessed the most powerful gust of wind ever recorded on land. The wind speed was measured at 231 miles per hour.

**More people have climbed Mount** Monadnock in New Hampshire than any other mountain in North America.

**On January 5, 1776, New Hampshire** became the first of the 13 colonies to declare its independence from Great Britain.

Portsmouth

**In 1800 the U.S. Navy chose the harbor** at Portsmouth, New Hampshire, for its first official naval shipyard.

**The first free public library in the world** opened in Peterborough, New Hampshire, in 1833. It was supported by tax money from the town and it was open to everyone.

**Skiing has long been a big part of** New Hampshire's winters. The state boasts the nation's first ski club (1872), first ski school (1929), first cleared ski trail (1930), and first overhead tow (1935).

# STATE SONG

New Hampshire has nine state songs. The official state song, "Old New Hampshire," was adopted in 1949. Over the years since then, the state legislature has adopted eight honorary state songs.

## OLD NEW HAMPSHIRE

*Words by Dr. John F. Holmes; music by Maurice Hoffmann*

With a skill that knows no meas-ure, From the gold-en store of Fate God, in

His great love and wis-dom, Made the rug-ged Gran-ite State; Made the

lakes, the fields, the for-ests; Make the riv-ers and the rills; Made the

bub-bling, crys-tal foun-tains of New Hamp-shire's Gran-ite Hills.

Old New Hamp-shire, Old New Hamp-shire, Old New Hamp-shire, grand and great, We will

sing of Old New Hamp-shire, Of the dear old Gran-ite State.

You can hear "Old New Hampshire" by visiting this website:
<http://www.50states.com/songs/newhamp.htm>

# A NEW HAMPSHIRE RECIPE

New Hampshire is well known for its delicious apples and sweet maple syrup. This easy-to-make recipe combines both of these tasty foods into one delicious breakfast. Ask for an adult's help with all steps using an oven or a knife.

## BAKED APPLE PANCAKE WITH PECANS AND MAPLE SYRUP

You will need:

1 cup pancake mix
½ cup milk
1 egg
2 tablespoons melted butter

1 cup peeled, cored, and sliced apples
½ teaspoon ground cinnamon
⅓ cup chopped pecans
3 tablespoons maple syrup

1. Preheat oven to 350° F.
2. Blend pancake mix, milk, and egg. Set aside.
3. Pour melted butter in nine-inch pie tin.
4. Place apple slices in bottom.
5. Sprinkle cinnamon and pecans over apples.
6. Drizzle syrup on top.
7. Pour batter over apples.
8. Bake at 350° F for 30 minutes, or until center of pancake is just firm.
9. Loosen pancake from hot pan. Set pancake upside down on plate, slice into wedges, and serve.

Makes one nine-inch pie-sized pancake.

# HISTORICAL TIMELINE

**9,000 B.C.** American Indians move into the New Hampshire area.

**A.D. 1614** Captain John Smith explores the New England coast for Britain.

**1622** King James I grants a large area of land in New England to Sir Ferdinando Gorges and John Mason.

**1629** John Mason gives New Hampshire its name.

**1680** New Hampshire becomes a separate British colony.

**1727** The city of Concord is founded.

**1763** The French and Indian War (1754–1763) ends with a British victory.

**1769** Dartmouth College is founded in Hanover.

**1776** New Hampshire adopts its own state constitution.

**1788** New Hampshire becomes the ninth state.

**1800** Portsmouth begins making ships for the U.S. Navy.

**1838** New Hampshire's first railroad, spanning between Nashua, New Hampshire, and Lowell, Massachusetts, is completed.

**1850** Daniel Webster helps pass the Compromise of 1850.

**1852** New Hampshirite Franklin Pierce is elected U.S. president.

**1861** The American Civil War begins; New Hampshire fights for the Union.

**1920** The Amoskeag textile mills in Manchester are the largest in the world.

**1922** Amoskeag workers stage a nine-month strike to protest wage cuts.

**1929** The first U.S. ski school opens near Franconia.

**1939** World War II (1939–1945) begins in Europe; New Hampshire manufactures equipment and materials for the Allied war effort.

**1963** New Hampshire begins operating the nation's first legal lottery since the 1800s.

**1990** The Christa McAuliffe Planetarium opens in Concord.

**1999** Hurricane Floyd hits the East Coast, causing flooding in three New Hampshire counties.

# OUTSTANDING NEW HAMPSHIRITES

**Alice Brown** (1856–1948) wrote short stories and plays describing the people and places of New Hampshire. Her works include *Meadow-Grass: Tales of New England Life* and *Children of Earth.* Brown was born in Hampton Falls, New Hampshire.

*Alice Brown*

**Ken Burns** (born 1953) is a documentary filmmaker who lives in New Hampshire. He has written, produced, and directed several films for public television, including *Jazz, The West, Baseball,* and *The Civil War.*

**Salmon P. Chase** (1808–1873), from Cornish, was secretary of the U.S. Treasury when, in 1863, he issued the first "greenbacks," or green dollar bills. He became the chief justice of the U.S. Supreme Court the next year. Chase often defended runaway slaves and supported giving free land to settlers in the West.

*Salmon P. Chase*

**Barbara Ann Cochran** (born 1951) is a skier from Claremont. Cochran won a gold medal for the women's slalom, a zigzag skiing event, in the 1972 Olympic Games.

**Mary Baker Eddy** (1821–1910) founded the Christian Science religion in 1879. In 1908 she started the daily newspaper the *Christian Science Monitor.* Eddy was born in Bow.

*Barbara Ann Cochran*

**William Pitt Fessenden** (1806–1869) was an influential politician in the 1800s. A founding member of the Republican Party, Fessenden served as a U.S. senator from 1854 to 1864 and again from 1865 to 1869. He was an important political leader during the Civil War.

*Mary Baker Eddy*

**Mike Flanagan** (born 1951) was a professional baseball pitcher from 1975 to 1995. In 1979, with the Baltimore Orioles, Flanagan led the American League in wins and won the Cy Young Award. Flanagan grew up in Manchester.

*Mike Flanagan*

**Elizabeth Gurley Flynn** (1890–1964), from Concord, New Hampshire, helped factory workers throughout the United States gain more rights and better working conditions. Flynn also helped found the American Civil Liberties Union, an organization dedicated to protecting the rights of all Americans.

*Daniel French*

**Sam Walter Foss** (1858–1911) was an editor, poet, and journalist. He is known for his portrayal of the speech of New Hampshirites. His most famous poem is "House by the Side of the Road."

**Daniel French** (1850–1931), from Exeter, New Hampshire, was a sculptor. He is remembered for his statues. One of his most famous statues is *Abraham Lincoln*, which stands in the Lincoln Memorial in Washington, D.C.

*Robert Frost*

**Robert Frost** (1874–1963) attended Dartmouth College in Hanover, New Hampshire, and later lived on farms in Derry and Franconia, New Hampshire. One of America's most-beloved poets, Frost wrote poems that celebrate nature and daily life in New England.

**Horace Greeley** (1811–1872), from Amherst, New Hampshire, founded and published the *New York Tribune*, a famous newspaper in the 1800s. In the paper, Greeley voiced his ideas and became an important political influence in America.

*Horace Greeley*

**Sarah Josepha Hale**

**Sarah Josepha Hale** (1788–1879), from Newport, New Hampshire, wrote and edited *Ladies Magazine* and *Godey's Lady's Book*. The magazines stressed pride and education for women. Hale also wrote several books and the nursery rhyme "Mary Had a Little Lamb."

**John Irving** (born 1942) is a best-selling author. His novels include *The World According to Garp, A Prayer for Owen Meany,* and *The Cider House Rules*. Irving was born in Exeter, New Hampshire.

**John Irving**

**Kancamagus** (1655?–1691?) was the last chief of the Pennacook Indians in New Hampshire. When war broke out between the British and the Indians, Kancamagus led his people to Canada to escape attacks. A highway in New Hampshire following that route is named after him.

**Christa McAuliffe** (1948–1986) was a New Hampshire schoolteacher. In 1985 she was selected by NASA to be the first civilian in space. On January 28, 1986, McAuliffe and the rest of the crew of the space shuttle *Challenger* were killed when the craft exploded seconds after takeoff.

**Bob Montana**

**Bob Montana** (1920–1975) created the comic strip "Archie" in 1942. The cartoons described the lives of American teenagers. Many of Montana's characters were based on classmates from his high school in Manchester.

**Maxfield Parrish** (1870–1966) illustrated hundreds of magazines and books, including *Mother Goose in Prose* and *The Arabian Nights*. The scenic area around Cornish, New Hampshire, where Parrish lived for much of his life, inspired many of his works.

**Maxfield Parrish**

**Franklin Pierce** (1804–1869), the 14th president of the United States, was born in Hillsboro, New Hampshire. One of Pierce's nicknames was Young Hickory of the Granite Hills.

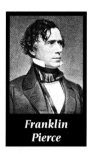

*Franklin Pierce*

**Eleanor Porter** (1868–1920), a children's author from Littleton, New Hampshire, wrote her way to fame with *Pollyanna.* The story sold over 1 million copies and was translated into many languages.

**Red Rolfe** (1908–1969), from Pennacook, New Hampshire, played and coached professional baseball. As the third baseman for the New York Yankees, Rolfe led the American League in 1939 with 213 hits and 139 runs.

*Red Rolfe*

**J. D. Salinger** (born 1919) lives near Cornish, New Hampshire. The author of many short stories, Salinger is most famous for his novel, *Catcher in the Rye.* The book is about the problems a teenage boy faces while growing up.

**Alan Shepard Jr.** (1923–1998) rocketed into space in 1961, becoming the first U.S. astronaut. In 1971 he commanded *Apollo 14* for the third moon landing in history and became the fifth astronaut to walk on the moon. Shepard is from East Derry, New Hampshire.

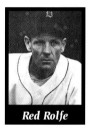

*Alan Shepard Jr.*

**David Souter** (born 1939) is an associate justice of the U.S. Supreme Court. He was appointed to the highest U.S. court in 1990. Justice Souter had previously served as a justice of the New Hampshire Supreme Court.

**Earl Tupper** (1907–1983) began selling the plastic storage containers he invented in 1945. Tupperware did not become popular until the 1950s, however, when sales skyrocketed at home parties. Tupper was born in Berlin, New Hampshire.

*Earl Tupper*

# FACTS-AT-A-GLANCE

**Nickname:** Granite State

**Song:** "Old New Hampshire"

**Motto:** Live Free or Die

**Flower:** purple lilac

**Tree:** white birch

**Bird:** purple finch

**Animal:** white-tailed deer

**Insect:** ladybug

**Mineral:** beryl

**Rock:** granite

**Date and ranking of statehood:**
    June 21, 1788, the ninth state

**Capital:** Concord

**Area:** 8,969 square miles

**Rank in area, nationwide:** 44th

**Average January temperature:** 19° F

**Average July temperature:** 68° F

New Hampshire's flag features the
state seal against a field of blue. The seal
is surrounded by nine stars, symbolizing
New Hampshire's place as the ninth state.

## POPULATION GROWTH

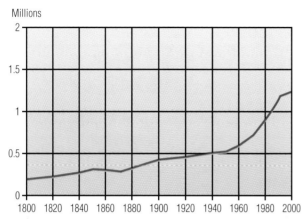

Millions

This chart shows how New Hampshire's population has grown from 1800 to 2000.

The *Raleigh,* a warship built at Portsmouth for use in the American Revolution, is pictured on New Hampshire's state seal.

**Population:** 1,235,786 (2000 census)

**Rank in population, nationwide:** 41st

**Major cities and populations:** (2000 census) Manchester (107,006), Nashua (86,605), Concord (40,687), Derry (34,021) Rochester (28,461)

**U.S. senators:** 2

**U.S. representatives:** 2

**Electoral votes:** 4

**Natural resources:** clay, feldspar, forests, granite, gravel, lakes, rivers, sand, soil

**Agricultural products:** apples, beef cattle, berries, Christmas trees, eggs, hay, maple syrup, milk, potatoes, poultry, sweet corn

**Manufactured goods:** computers, electric lamps, electronics equipment, leather, lumber and wood products, metals, paper products, plastics

## WHERE NEW HAMPSHIRITES WORK

**Services**—66 percent (services includes jobs in trade; community, social, and personal services; finance, insurance, and real estate; transportation, communication, and utilities)

**Manufacturing**—15 percent

**Government**—11 percent

**Construction**—6 percent

**Agriculture**—2 percent

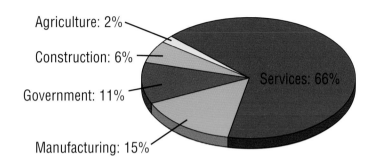

Agriculture: 2%
Construction: 6%
Government: 11%
Services: 66%
Manufacturing: 15%

## GROSS STATE PRODUCT

**Services**—64 percent

**Manufacturing**—23 percent

**Government**—9 percent

**Construction**—3 percent

**Agriculture**—1 percent

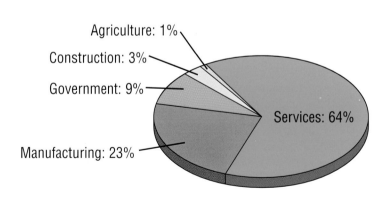

Agriculture: 1%
Construction: 3%
Government: 9%
Services: 64%
Manufacturing: 23%

# STATE WILDLIFE

**Mammals:** beaver, black bear, chipmunk, deer, fox, mink, moose, rabbit, raccoon, skunk, squirrel

**Birds:** bluebird, duck, goose, pheasant, purple finch, robin, ruffed grouse, sparrow, warbler, woodcock

**Amphibians and reptiles:** bullfrog, garter snake, frog, milk snake, mudpuppy, newt, ringneck snake, salamander, snapping turtle, spotted turtle, timber rattlesnake, toad, wood turtle

**Fish:** bass, bluefish, bullhead, cod, cunner, cusk, flounder, haddock, hake, mackerel, perch, pickerel, pollock, salmon, striped bass, trout, tuna, whitefish

**Trees:** ash, basswood, beech, birch, cedar, elm, fir, hemlock, maple, oak, pine, spruce, tamarack

**Wild plants:** American elder, black-eyed Susan, blueberry, daisy, fireweed, gentian, goldenrod, mountain laurel, purple trillium, sumac, violet, wild aster

Spotted salamander

# PLACES TO VISIT

**Cathedral of the Pines, Rindge**
This national memorial to American men and women who died in service to their country is also an outdoor inter-denominational church.

**Christa McAuliffe Planetarium, Concord**
Named after the Concord schoolteacher and astronaut who died in the space shuttle *Challenger* explosion in 1986, the planetarium uses computer graphics, special effects, and sound to bring the solar system, constellations, and space exploration to life.

The Christa McAuliffe Planetarium in Concord

**Flume Gorge, Franconia Notch State Park**
An 800-foot-long natural chasm (deep, narrow valley), the Flume offers a scenic wilderness tour that features rare and beautiful mountain flowers.

**Hampton Beach, Hampton**
Vacationers and residents alike enjoy one of New England's finest beaches. The beach hosts numerous activities throughout the summer, including free live music, para-sailing, fireworks, and talent shows.

**The Isles of Shoals, 10 miles off the coast**
These nine islands (four belong to New Hampshire, five to Maine) have a fascinating history of piracy, ghosts, and other legends. Cruises, river trips, and whale-watching expeditions are available from May through October.

## Lake Winnipesaukee, Lakes Region

Featuring 283 miles of shoreline and 274 islands, Winnipesaukee ("Smile of the Great Spirit") is New Hampshire's largest lake. During summer, the lake is enjoyed by sightseers, boaters, fishers, and other water-sports enthusiasts.

## Mount Washington, White Mountains Region

The highest mountain in the northeastern United States (6,288 feet) features hiking and scenic drives in the summer, and cross-country skiing and snowshoeing in the winter.

## Old Man of the Mountain (Great Stone Face), near Franconia

New Hampshire's most famous landmark, this rocky cliff looks like an old man's face. The unusual rock formation was made famous by the Nathaniel Hawthorne short story "The Great Stone Face."

## Strawbery Banke Museum, Portsmouth

A restored colonial seaport, Strawbery Banke is named after the wild strawberries English settlers found in the area. The 10-acre museum features gardens, exhibits, and craft shops, as well as 46 buildings constructed between 1695 and 1820.

## Wildcat Mountain Ski Area, near Pinkham Notch

One of the best spots for skiing in the White Mountains region, Wildcat Mountain features some very challenging downhill runs for experts, as well as courses for skiers of all ages and levels of ability.

# ANNUAL EVENTS

World Championship Sled Dog Derby, Laconia—*February*

Wildquack River Festival, Jackson—*May*

Annual Crafts Festival, Portsmouth—*June*

Monadnock Balloon and Aviation Festival, on Mount Monadnock—*June*

Frost Day, Franconia—*July*

Annual Teddy Bear Clinic, Portsmouth—*August*

Children's Festival, Hampton Beach—*August*

World Championships Mud Bowl, North Conway—*September*

Annual Seafood Festival, Hampton Beach—*September*

Olde New England Foliage Festival, Barrington—*October*

Annual Railfest, North Conway—*October*

Northern Lights Festival, Waterville Valley—*November*

Candlelight Stroll, Portsmouth—*December*

# LEARN MORE ABOUT NEW HAMPSHIRE

## BOOKS

### General

Otfinoski, Steve. *New Hampshire.* Tarrytown, NY: Benchmark Books, 1999. For older readers.

Stein, R. Conrad. *New Hampshire.* New York: Children's Press, 2000. For older readers.

Whitehurst, Susan. *The Colony of New Hampshire.* New York: The Rosen Publishing Group, Inc., 2000.

### Special Interest

Bober, Natalie S. *A Restless Spirit: The Story of Robert Frost.* New York: Henry Holt, 1998. Biography of New Hampshire native and beloved American poet Robert Frost.

Goldstein, Ernest. *The Statue* Abraham Lincoln, *A Masterpiece by Daniel Chester French.* Minneapolis, MN: Lerner Publications Company, 1997. The story of the creation of Daniel Chester French's statue of Abraham Lincoln that sits within the Lincoln Memorial in Washington, D.C.

Lurie, Jon. *Fundamental Snowboarding.* Minneapolis, MN: Lerner Publications Company, 1996. This book is all about snowboarding, a very popular sport on New Hampshire's many slopes.

## Fiction

Blos, Joan W. *A Gathering of Days: A New England Girl's Journal, 1830-32.* New York: Simon and Schuster, 1979. For older readers. In this 1980 Newbery Medal winner, teenager Catherine describes daily life on a New Hampshire farm. She faces difficult changes when her widowed father remarries and a friend dies.

Bruchac, Joseph. *The Heart of a Chief.* New York: Dial Books for Young Readers, 1998. An 11-year-old Pennacook Indian boy living on a fictional New Hampshire reservation faces his father's alcoholism, a controversy surrounding plans for a casino on a tribal island, and insensitivity toward Native Americans in his school and nearby town.

Curry, Jane Louise. *Moon Window.* New York: Margaret McElderry Books, 1996. Set in New Hampshire, this supernatural story follows a girl who can travel through time by climbing through a window.

Frost, Robert. *Robert Frost: Poetry for Young People.* New York: Sterling Publishing Company, 1994. A collection of poems about the four seasons by the famous New Hampshire poet.

# WEBSITES

**New Hampshire State Government Online**
<http://www.state.nh.us/>
New Hampshire's official state website has links to executive, legislative, and judicial branches of New Hampshire government, as well as a New Hampshire almanac.

**The Official Site of the New Hampshire Division of Travel and Tourism Development**
<http://www.visitnh.gov/>
The state's official tourism site has information on events, lodging and dining, tour information, and New Hampshire facts.

**The Online Edition of *The Union Leader* and *New Hampshire Sunday News***
< http://www.theunionleader.com/>
The online version of New Hampshire's largest daily newspapers covers national, state, and local news.

# PRONUNCIATION GUIDE

**Amoskeag** (am-uh-SKAY-uhg)

**Androscoggin** (an-druh-SKAWG-uhn)

**Exeter** (EHK-suht-ur)

**Gorges, Ferdinando** (GOR-jehz, fir-dih-NAHN-doh)

**Monadnock** (muh-NAD-nahk)

**Nashua** (NASH-uh-wuh)

**Pemigewasset** (pehm-ih-juh-WAHS-uht)

**Pennacook** (pehn-uh-kook)

**Piscataqua** (pihs-KAT-uh-kwaw)

**Portsmouth** (PORT-smuth)

**Winnipesaukee** (wihn-uh-puh-SAW-kee)

# GLOSSARY

**colony:** a territory ruled by a country some distance away

**constitution:** the system of basic laws or rules of a government, society, or organization; the document in which these laws or rules are written

**development:** the buildup of homes, office buildings, factories, and roads upon land that once was wild. Human activities, such as mining and logging, which remove things from the land also are types of development.

**glacier:** a large body of ice and snow that moves slowly over land

**hydropower:** the electricity produced by using the forces of flowing water; also called hydroelectric power

**immigrant:** a person who moves into a foreign country and settles there

**lava:** hot, melted rock that erupts from a volcano or from cracks in the earth's surface and that hardens as it cools

**precipitation:** rain, snow, hail, and other forms of moisture that fall to earth

**reservoir:** a place where water is collected and stored for later use

# INDEX

# PHOTO ACKNOWLEDGMENTS

Cover photographs by © Darrell Gulin/CORBIS (left) and © Phil Schermeister/COR-BIS (right); PresentationMaps.com, pp. 1, 8, 9, 45; © Kevin Fleming/CORBIS, pp. 2–3, 40; © Robert Maass/CORBIS, p. 3; © M. Angelo/CORBIS, pp. 4 (detail), 7 (detail), 17 (detail), 39 (detail), 51 (detail); Tony LaGruth, pp. 6, 12; © Roger Treadwell/Visuals Unlimited, p. 7; David Brownell/State of New Hampshire, p. 11 (top); © Phil Schermeister/CORBIS, pp. 11 (right), 50; © Makonny T. Titlow/Visuals Unlimited, p. 13; Craig Blouin, pp. 14, 39, 41, 48, 52 (right), 53, 54, 55 (both), 56, 61, 80; © Karlene V. Schwartz, pp. 15, 43 (left), 51, 58; © Will Troyer/Visuals Unlimited, p. 16 (left); © Gerry Lemmo, pp. 16 (right), 18, 23, 43 (right), 44; Hillel Burger, Peabody Museum, Harvard University, p. 19; National Museum of the American Indian/Smithsonian Institution, neg. no. 14656, p. 20; Virginia State Library and Archives, p. 21; New Hampshire Historical Society, pp. 22 (#F411), 25 (G790), 28 (#F3551), 30 (#G370), 37 (#N14HS242); Independent Picture Service, pp. 24, 29, 32; © John D. Cunningham/Visuals Unlimited, p. 27; Dartmouth College Library, pp. 31, 68 (bottom), 69 (second from top); © James Blank/Root Resources, p. 33; Museum of American Textile History, p. 35; © CORBIS, pp. 36, 38; © John Kohout/Root Resources, p. 42; Sharon Callahan, League of New Hampshire Craftsmen, p. 46 (left); New Hampshire Department of Agriculture, pp. 46 (right), 49; B. Alexander, League of New Hampshire Craftsmen, p. 47; New Hampshire Department of Environmental Services, p. 52 (left); © Nubar Alexanian/CORBIS, p. 57; New Hampshire Fish and Game, p. 59; George Karn, p. 60; Tim Seeley, pp. 63, 71 (top), 72; Boston Athenaeum, p. 66 (top); Library of Congress, pp. 66 (second from top and bottom), 67 (second from top and bottom), 69 (top); © Bettmann/CORBIS, p. 66 (second from bottom); National Baseball Library Cooperstown, NY, p. 67 (top); Courtesy of the Jones Library, Inc., Amherst, MA, Reprinted by permission of the Estate of Robert Frost, p. 67 (second from bottom); Dictionary of American Portraits, p. 68 (top); © Rune Hellestad/CORBIS, p. 68 (second from top); Montana Family, p. 68 (second from bottom); NASA, p. 69 (second from bottom); Tupperware Home Parties, p. 69 (bottom); © Lynda Richardson/CORBIS, p. 73; Lynn Rice, p. 74.